The Gunniwolf

Illustrated by William Wiesner

The Gunniwolf

Retold by Wilhelmina Harper

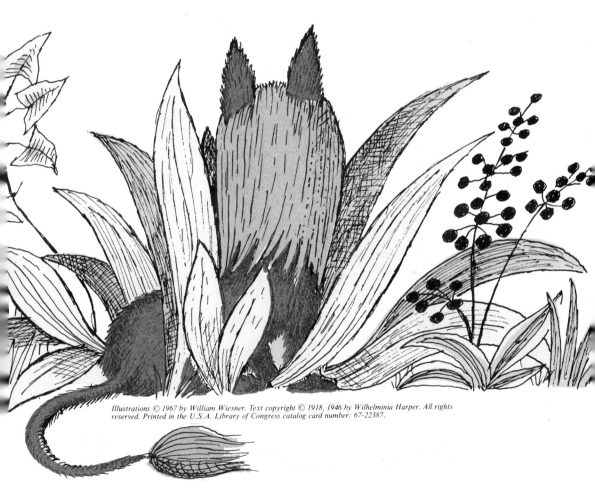

E. P. Dutton New York

C 2

T here was once a little girl who lived with her mother very close to a dense jungle. Each day the mother would caution Little Girl to be most careful and never enter the jungle, because—if she did—the Gunniwolf might get her! Little Girl always promised that she would never, NEVER even go NEAR the jungle.

One day the mother had to go away for a while. Her last words were to caution Little Girl that whatever else she did she must keep far away from the jungle! And Little Girl was very sure that she would not go anywhere *near* it.

The mother was hardly out of sight, however, when Little Girl noticed some beautiful white flowers growing at the very edge of the jungle. "Oh," she thought, "wouldn't I love to have some of those—I'll pick just a few."

Then, forgetting all about the warning, she began to gather the white flowers, all the while singing happily to herself:

"Kum-kwa, khi-wa,

kum kwa, khi-wa."

All of a sudden she noticed, a little further in the jungle, some beautiful *pink* flowers growing. "Oh," she thought, "I must surely gather some of those too!"

On she tripped, farther into the jungle, and began picking the pink flowers, all the while singing happily:

"Kum-kwa, khi-wa,

kum-kwa, khi-wa."

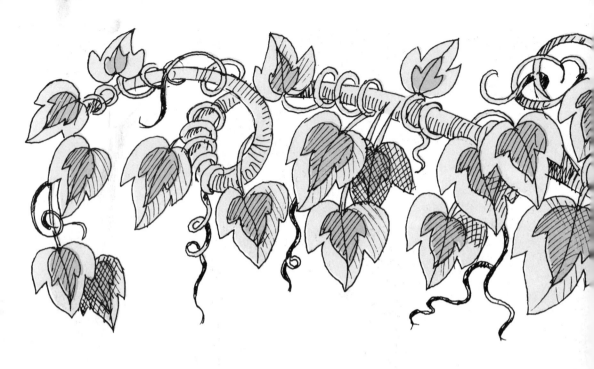

When she had her arms full of white and pink flowers, she peeped a little further, and way in the middle of the jungle she saw some beautiful *orange* flowers growing. "Oh," she thought, "I'll take just a few of those, and what a pretty bouquet I'll have to show my mother!"

So she gathered the orange flowers too, singing to herself all the while:

"Kum-kwa, khi-wa,

kum-kwa, khi-wa—"

when SUDDENLY—up rose the Gunniwolf!

He said, "Little Girl, why for you move?"

Tremblingly she answered, "I no move."

The Gunniwolf said, "Then you sing that guten sweeten song again!"

So she sang:

"Kum-kwa, khi-wa,

kum-kwa, khi-wa"

and then—the old Gunniwolf nodded his head and fell fast asleep.

Away ran Little Girl as fast as ever she could:

pit-pat,   pit-pat,   pit-pat.

               pit-pat,   pit-pat,